CROONER
Legends

WRITTEN BY
David Curnock

This edition first published in the UK in 2007
By Green Umbrella Publishing

© Green Umbrella Publishing 2007

www.greenumbrella.co.uk

Publishers: Jules Gammond and Vanessa Gardner

Printed and bound in China

ISBN: 978-1-905828-72-2

The views in this book are those of the author but they are general views only and readers are urged to consult the relevant and qualified specialist
for individual advice in particular situations.

Green Umbrella Publishing hereby exclude all liability to the extent permitted by law of any errors or omissions in this book and for any loss, damage
or expense (whether direct or indirect) suffered by a third party relying on any information contained in this book.

All our best endeavours have been made to secure copyright clearance for every photograph used but in the event of any copyright owner being overlooked
please address correspondence to Green Umbrella Publishing, The Old Bakehouse, 21 The Street, Lydiard Millicent, Swindon SN5 3LU

CROONER

Legends

CROONER
Legends

CONTENTS

CROONER *Legends*

CONTENTS

CROONER *Legends*

FREDASTAIRE

Birth name: Frederick Austerlitz

Born: May 10 1899, Omaha, Nebraska

Died: June 22 1987

Years active: 1905 – 1981

Record label(s): RCA Victor, Brunswick, Columbia, Decca, Mercury, Verve, Kapp Records, United Artists

P erhaps best known as a song and dance man, as the result of his vaudeville background and a series of screen musicals starring alongside Ginger Rogers, the elegant Fred Astaire was a respected crooner in his own right. Although he often claimed he could not sing, he introduced some classic hits from The Great American Songbook that have stood the test of time. Without achieving the volume of record sales as some, he nevertheless brought great songs to the fore with his distinctive vocalisation of hits such as, "Night and Day" and "Cheek to Cheek."

Fred Astaire was born Frederick Austerlitz in Omaha, Nebraska, on May 10 1899. His father, Frederic Austerlitz, was an immigrant from Austria who worked as a salesman for the Storz Brewing Company. Fred's father played the piano and was fascinated with the world of show business, as was his mother, Johanna. The daughter of the family, Adele Marie, was almost two years older than Fred and, when she was six, enrolled in a dancing academy. In 1905, the family moved to New York after a temperance movement had caused the brewery to shut down. The family, soon to adopt the surname Astaire that was believed to come from an uncle, duly enrolled Adele in a dancing school with an eye to her future career prospects. Fred soon joined her as part of a dance act that went on to make its professional debut in Keyport, New Jersey, in November 1905 when Adele was eight years old, and young Fred was six.

With varying degrees of success, their vaudeville career continued, eventually making it onto Broadway in 1917 with Over The Top. Fred had already made acquaintance with George Gershwin, who was working as a song plugger. More shows followed and, with increasing acclaim, they rose to the top of the bill. A flop show in 1923 saw them move to England to appear in the West End in *Top Flirting*, and also record their first UK only release, for HMV, with two songs from the show. On returning to New York, they starred in the Gershwin smash hit *Lady Be Good* that ran for 330 performances, followed by another 336 when they brought it to London. Back in the US, another hit show, *Funny Face* was also brought to the UK in 1928, where it repeated its success.

In 1932, Adele gave up her career to marry Charles Cavendish, son of the Duke of Devonshire. Fred continued his stage and recording career as a solo act, recording "Night And Day" in 1933. He was soon given a screen test that, in spite of being criticised for his looks, led to a film contract with RKO. This led to a legendary cinematic pairing with Ginger Rogers in 10 musicals. Astaire recorded many of the hit songs from the films,

CROONER *Legends*

among these were, "Cheek to Cheek," "No Strings," "Isn't This a Lovely Day?" "Top Hat, White Tie and Tails," and "The Piccolino." By the end of the 30s the films were losing money so the partnership with Ginger was ended. Fred made films for several studios, and continued recording, before signing a long-term deal with MGM. His 1946 recording of "Puttin' on the Ritz" from the hit film *Blue Skies*, reached No 2 in the *Billboard* charts.

At the age of 47, Fred decided to give up dancing to concentrate on owning and breeding horses. Gene Kelly broke his ankle just before filming was due to start on *Easter Parade* so Astaire was asked to deputise. His retirement had lasted less than a year, and Fred continued working on films, radio and television. The 1958 one-hour special *An Evening with Fred Astaire* won him nine Emmy awards. Serious film acting, notably his performance in *On The Beach*, and his role in the musical *Finian's Rainbow* took care of the 1960s, with more film and television work keeping him busy into his 70s. In 1975 he made three LPs in England for United Artists, and the following year saw Fred making more films and television movies, earning him his third Emmy Award for Outstanding Actor in a Special.

At the age of 78, Fred broke his wrist while playing around on his grandson's skateboard; this event brought him lifelong membership of the National Skateboard Society. Twice married, the first in 1933 to the Boston socialite Phyllis Potter with whom he had two children, Fred Jr, born in 1936, and Ava, born in 1942. Phyllis died from cancer in 1955, when Fred was making the film *Daddy Long Legs*. His second marriage, in 1980, was to Robyn Smith, an actress turned jockey, almost 45 years his junior. On his death from pneumonia, in 1987, it was revealed that one of Fred's last requests was to thank his fans for their support.

CROONER *Legends*

9

TONY BENNETT

Birth name: Anthony Dominick Benedetto
Born: August 3 1926, Queens, New York
Years active: 1936 – present
Record label(s): Columbia, MGM Records, Improv (Bennett's own label)

O ften referred to as The Singer's Singer, Tony Bennett has many admirers. In a 1965 interview for Life magazine, Frank Sinatra said, "For my money, Tony Bennett is the best singer in the business. He excites me when I watch him. He moves me. He's the singer who gets across what the composer has in mind, and probably a little more."

Anthony Dominick Benedetto was born, and grew up, in the Astoria neighbourhood of Queens, in New York City. His father, a grocer, died when Tony was 10 years old, leaving his seamstress mother to support her family. The youngster spent much of his spare time drawing pictures in chalk, on the sidewalks around his home. At the age of 10, his vocal talent was highlighted when he sang at the opening ceremony of the Triborough Bridge in 1936. By his teens, he was already set on a career as a professional singer. After briefly studying art, he left to help support the family, working as a singing waiter in Italian restaurants. Drafted into the US Army at 18, Bennett served as an infantryman on the front line in France and Germany, and later sang with an army band, using the name Joe Bari.

After the war, Bennett studied singing, learning the Italian *bel canto* voice discipline, while still working as a waiter. His interest in jazz led him to vocally mimic the phrasing of jazz musicians. His improvisational ability earned him a place in singer Pearl Bailey's 1949 show, in Greenwich Village, to which Bob Hope had been invited. Hope invited Bennett to join his touring show, but advised him to drop the name Bari. In 1950, Bennett made a demonstration disc, and was duly signed for Columbia Records. His first big hit, "Because of You," sold over a million copies, and was in the charts for 10 weeks, reaching the No 1 position in 1951.

His 1952 marriage to Patricia Beech dismayed his female fans; around 2,000 of them, wearing mourning black, had gathered outside St Patrick's Cathedral, New York, for the ceremony. The couple had two sons, D'Andrea (known as Danny) and Daegal, shortened to Dae, both of whom would become important influences in Bennett's later career. A third No 1 hit, "Rags to Riches," topped the charts for eight weeks in 1953. International fame was achieved when his record "Stranger in Paradise," from the show *Kismet*, reached No 1 in both America and Britain. Even during the downturn that coincided with the rock era in the late 1950s, Tony was able to achieve eight *Billboard* Top 40 entries.

When pianist Ralph Sharon became his musical director in 1957, Bennett made a highly acclaimed, jazz-orientated LP, *Beat of My Heart*. Collaboration with Count Basie led

CROONER *Legends*

CROONER *Legends*

to two more successful albums, *Basie Swings, Bennett Sings*, in 1958, and *In Person!* which featured the song "Chicago," in 1959. His reputation soared, culminating in a sold-out concert at Carnegie Hall in 1962. That year he recorded his signature song, the double *Grammy*-winning, "I Left My Heart in San Francisco." It stayed in various charts for a year but, surprisingly, only made No 19 in the *Billboard* Hot 100. Apart from another Top 5 album, his parting company with Ralph Sharon in 1965 coupled with the rise of Beatlemania sent Tony's career into decline.

Divorced in 1971, Tony married Sandra Grant in 1972 with whom he had two daughters, Joanna and Antonia. His recording label, Improv, had some success with two albums and the single "What Is This Thing Called Love?" before failing in 1977. By 1979, he had no recording contract and, in 1980, was divorced. Drug addiction took hold and, in desperation, he called his sons for help. Danny, a good businessman, became his manager and moved him back to New York, to sing in smaller venues. Re-united with Ralph Sharon, he signed for Columbia in 1986 and reached the charts with his album *The Art of Excellence*. Gradually, his career recovered; his albums *Astoria: Portrait of the Artist* (1990), the Sinatra tribute *Perfectly Frank* (1992), and his Astaire collection *Steppin' Out* (1993), with the latter two going gold and winning *Grammys*, firmly placed the artist back at the top. In 1995, his *MTV Unplugged* was *Grammy* Album of the Year.

Inducted into the Big Band and Jazz Hall of Fame in 1997, Tony Bennett has a star on the Hollywood Walk of Fame. Still touring, Bennett has made some of his most memorable albums in recent years. An accomplished painter, as Anthony Benedetto, an example of his art is displayed in the Smithsonian American Art Museum, Washington DC.

In August 2006, at the age of 80, Bennett made his album *Duets: An American Classic*, a fine example of his timeless vocal craft. His warm, slightly husky, tenor voice with its distinctive timbre remains instantly recognisable after 60 years of song.

LEFT
Tony Bennett performing on stage with Jazz drummer Art Blakey.

BELOW
Tony Bennett singing at the Royal Command Performance, 1965.

CROONER*Legends*

PAT**BOONE**

Birth name: Charles Eugene Patrick Boone

Born: June 1 1934, Jacksonville, Florida

Years active: 1954 – 2000s

Record label(s): Republic Records, Dot, London, Rediffusion (in the UK), Hip-O Records, The Gold Label

A singer who came to the fore during the 1950s, Pat Boone has crossed over several musical boundaries. From popular ballads, R&B, country and gospel, he has blended chameleon-like against different musical backgrounds, as well as standing out in front of others. His, at times, outspoken political and racial views seem at odds with his religious upbringing and family background.

Charles Eugene Patrick Boone, better known as Pat Boone, was born in Jacksonville, Florida, on June 1 1934. He is, reportedly, a direct descendant of the famous American pioneer, Daniel Boone. When he was two years old, his family moved to Nashville, Tennessee, where he spent his childhood. Pat attended David Lipscomb College, a Church of Christ sponsored private high school, now a university, in Nashville. He started singing, professionally, while a student at North Texas State College in Denton, Texas. In 1953, while only 19, he married Shirley Lee Foley, daughter of country music star Red Foley. The Boones, who have remained married ever since, are parents to four daughters, Cherry, Lindy, Debby, and Laury. His daughter Debby has followed a career in music, and had the *Grammy* winning, top-selling US single in 1977 with "You Light Up My Life."

Recording for Republic Records from 1954, he had a massive hit with a cover of "Ain't That a Shame," outselling the Fats Domino original. Remaining in the R&B cover business for the early years of his recording career, Boone made the music of many black performers more acceptable to the white population during the civil rights problems in the US at that period. Although he made six hit R&B covers, including that of Fats Domino, only four were rock songs including "Tutti Frutti" and "Long Tall Sally," previously hits for Little Richard. The two blues ballads, "I Almost Lost My Mind" and, "Chains of Love," the latter a hit for both Big Joe Turner and BB King, set Pat Boone straight down the middle-of-the-road, musically. Following in the footsteps of his idol, Bing Crosby, he scored several massive hits with ballads such as, "Love Letters in the Sand," "April Love," "Friendly Persuasion" and "Don't Forbid Me."

Boone became something of a style icon to the American teenagers, with his clean-cut, wholesome appearance and trademark white buckskin shoes, and was second only to Elvis Presley in popularity. He appeared in several films, most notably *April Love* in 1957, *Journey to the Center of the Earth* (1960), and *State Fair* (1962) in which he made his only on-screen kiss. He also wrote the theme music for the film *Exodus*. Pat also hosted a networked television series late in the 50s. His last Top 40 hit, in 1962, was the novelty

CROONER *Legends*

record "Speedy Gonzales." As musical tastes changed, Pat moved toward the country music and gospel sections in the record stores, as well as performing in radio. He and his family also took to the road to tour with a gospel show in the 1960s and 70s.

It has been well documented that Boone is a devout Christian, brought up and partly educated in the Church of Christ. His moral standards were often at odds with the demands of show business, causing him to decline work that he believed would compromise his religious beliefs. Born-again, Pat has been a member of the Pentecostal church for over 30 years. With their home in Los Angeles, Pat and Shirley still attend church regularly.

A previous neighbour of the Boones was the rock singer, Ozzy Osbourne, formerly lead singer with Black Sabbath. Pat made a cover version of Osbourne's hit song "Crazy Train" that became the theme song for *The Osbournes,* a reality documentary TV series. Ozzy reportedly said that Boone had never complained about living next door to his unconventional family.

In recent times, Pat has become a disc jockey on radio, and runs his own record label that specialises in new recordings by former great artists from the past who no longer interest the major labels. His company, The Gold Label - Honest Entertainment, releases records made by singers of the calibre of Jack Jones, Glen Campbell, Patty Page, Cleo Laine, The Four Freshmen, and Roger Williams, as well as the proprietor himself. In 1997, Pat released an album of heavy metal covers that he performed in his own style, *Metal Mood: No More Mr Nice Guy.* His achievements in gospel music were recognised in 2003, when he was inducted into the Gospel Music Hall of Fame.

In August 2006, he wrote an article for the online periodical *WorldNetDaily* in support of actor Mel Gibson, who had allegedly made anti-Semitic remarks. Pat Boone is a fervent patriot and, in a series of articles for that journal, his patriotism comes alive, as he writes with enthusiasm and sincerity.

CROONER *Legends*

MICHAEL BUBLÉ

Birth name: Michael Steven Bublé

Born: September 9 1975, Burnaby, Vancouver, Canada

Years active: 1988 – present

Record label(s): 143 Records/Reprise Records, Warner Elektra Atlantic (Italy)

"It was my Grandfather Mitch who is still my best friend who introduced me to this kind of music. He would play a record of Sinatra, Dean Martin, Ella Fitzgerald, Bing Crosby or the Mills Brothers on an old record player. I never saw these singers on stage, I only listened to their music but everything I was going to learn I pretty much learned by listening to the lifetime's work of these artists." So said Michael, recalling his early musical memories.

The eldest of three children, Michael Steven Bublé was born in a suburb of Vancouver BC, Canada, on September 9 1975. He has two sisters, Brandee and Crystal. Michael is very proud of his Italian family origins; he is particularly proud of his Italian grandfather, Demetrio Santagata, known as Mitch, who captured young Michael's interest in the jazz and ballad singers from the golden years of song. By the age of five the Bing Crosby hit, "White Christmas" was being sung by the youngster, many times over and often out of season, around the house. Michael's singing talent was obvious from the age of 13, when he entered, and won, a local talent contest. However, he was disqualified for being underage; he was compensated four years later, when he won first prize at the nationwide Canadian Youth Talent Search.

In his teens, and while still at high school, Bublé sang in hotels and clubs in the evenings and at weekends, and occasionally helped out on his father's salmon fishing boat. In order to obtain the club and hotel bookings, his grandfather Mitch, a plumber, offered to carry out plumbing work at the venues in return for the proprietors allowing his protégé to perform. When he was 17, Michael took lessons from voice coaches. He was soon offered work on the Red Rock Diner Roadshow that was organised by a Vancouver 'retro' radio station, and toured throughout the US; part of his act was an impression of Elvis Presley. His future girlfriend, Debbie Timuss, also appeared on the show although it has been claimed that they first met while both were in a musical review, *Forever Swing.*

In 1996, Michael recorded the first of three independent albums, *First Dance*, which was made for his grandfather, and not released. In the next three years or so, the Bublé career was marking time, with him recording demo discs, appearing in minor television shows, and singing at a series of small gigs that failed to swell his bank balance by any large degree. He had considered the prospect of leaving show business entirely, as he could see no way forward. His second independent album was *Babalu,* recorded in 2001, but not a great commercial success. However, its first track, "Spiderman Theme," was re-mixed and used as the theme tune for the film. His third independent album, in 2002, was entitled *Dream.*

CROONER *Legends*

In September 2000, Michael was singing at a corporate engagement where he met a person who, unknown to him at the time, was to have a profound impact on his future career. Michael gave the man one of his CDs and told him that, if he did not like it, it could be used as a beer mat. The following day, the man called him on the phone and told Michael that he was an aide to no less a person than Brian Mulroney, the former Prime Minister of Canada. He asked Bublé to perform at the wedding celebrations after the marriage of Mulroney's daughter, Caroline. The aide also told him that David Foster, the head of the American label 143 Records would be attending and would like Michael to sing for him. This resulted in the signing of a recording contract with Foster's company, a subsidiary of Atlantic Records. Early in 2001, Bublé went to Los Angeles to start work on his first major-label album that would be released through Reprise Records.

LEFT
Michael Bublé
performing in 2006.

BELOW
Bublé in rehearsal,
Australia 2005.

The album *Michael Bublé* reportedly took nine months to make, and was not released until February 2003. Featuring a range of standards including "Fever," "Sway," "Come Fly With Me" and "That's All," the album was an instant success. Within a year, it sold over 2 million copies world-wide, over half a million in the UK alone, and went double platinum in Australia. It reached No 9 in the charts in the land of his forefathers, Italy. His 2004 live video album, *Come Fly With Me*, made it into the Top 10 of *Billboard* Music Video Charts, and went platinum, in the year he was given a Juno Award in Canada, for being the Artist of the Year. His 2005 studio album, *It's Time*, the first of his albums available for internet download, went double platinum in the US, and has sold more than 5 million copies world-wide.

NAT
KINGCOLE

Birth name: Nathaniel Adams Coles
Born: March 17 1919, Montgomery, Alabama
Died: February 15 1965, Santa Monica, California
Years active: Mid-1930s to 1964
Record label(s): Capitol

Official US census records show that Nathaniel Adams Coles was born in Montgomery, Alabama on St Patrick's Day 1919, although he claimed on various documents to have been born in 1915, 1916, 1917 and 1919. The eldest child of Edward James Coles and Perlina Adams Coles, he was brought up in the Bronzeville district of Chicago. His family was understandably very religious, partly due to his father's calling as a pastor, and the fact that his mother was the daughter of a Baptist minister. Although his father was against popular music, Nat's mother, herself a capable organist, encouraged him to play the piano from an early age. He took formal lessons from the age of 12, and his repertoire expanded to cover not only jazz and gospel music, but also the classical works of Bach and Rachmaninoff.

In his teens, Perlina persuaded Edward to allow their son to play jazz, in return for him providing the music at the pastor's Sunday services. His passion for jazz led him to hanging around outside clubs where artists such as Louis Armstrong and his particular idol, Earl 'Fatha' Hines, played. Nat soon began performing, with his older brother Eddie Coles playing the bass, in their own band in jazz clubs where he acquired his appellation, 'King', presumably from the Old King Cole rhyme; somewhere along the way he dropped the 's' from his surname.

The band made their first recording in 1936, under Eddie's name. The next step on Nat's career ladder was as pianist on a touring revue *Shuffle Along*, but this show failed while on the road in Long Beach, California, where Nat decided to remain. His career moved away from his jazz roots around the early 1940s and, although he was accused of selling out, his move into mainstream popular music was to prove a very successful, and profitable, transition. His first popular hit was a recording of the self-penned "Straighten Up and Fly Right," based on a folk story used in a sermon by his father. The record was released by Capitol and sold over 500,000 copies, thus beginning a long association with that label.

Another of his greatest mainstream offerings was "The Christmas Song," which he recorded three times: first in 1946, then in 1953 when he incorrectly sang "reindeers", and again in 1961, probably the most-played version. With a string of hits in the late 1940s and early 1950s, including "Nature Boy," "Mona Lisa," "Too Young," and the aptly-named "Unforgettable" that became his signature tune, it was claimed that Nat's success financed the building of Capitol Records' distinctive circular headquarters building at

CROONER *Legends*

Vine Street, Los Angeles. Known to many as 'The House that Nat Built', it was the first building of its type in the US, when constructed in 1956.

In 1948, Nat bought a house in the hitherto all-white Hancock Park district of Los Angeles. The local property owners association made it clear to Cole that they did not want any undesirables moving in, to which Cole reportedly replied, "Neither do I. And if I see anybody undesirable coming in here, I'll be the first to complain." In this period in America the problem of racial difference was ongoing; on one occasion Nat was attacked, in a possible kidnap attempt, while on stage in Birmingham, Alabama, leading to his decision to never appear in the Deep South again. It also sparked his political activities. His networked television programme *The Nat King Cole Show*, in December 1957, the first TV show to be hosted by an African-American, closed down due to the reluctance by national companies to invest their sponsorship. Nat claimed that, "Madison Avenue is afraid of the dark." Having previously spoken at the 1956 Republican Convention, Cole switched to the Democrats, supporting the campaign of the future President, John F Kennedy. In office, JFK and his successor, Lyndon Johnson, both frequently consulted Nat on civil rights issues.

His first marriage to Nadine Robinson, in 1936, ended in divorce in 1948. In almost indecent haste, some nine days later, he married Maria (born Marie) Hawkins, whose stage name was Maria Ellington, a singer with the Duke Ellington band. Their family included the adopted Carol, known as Cookie, daughter of Maria's youngest sister who died, in 1949. Their first natural child Natalie was born in 1950: she later became a moderately successful singer in her own right. In 1959, Nat and Maria adopted a boy, Kelly, followed in January 1961 by the birth of natural twin girls, Casey and Timolin. Nat's serial affairs plagued their marriage but Maria stayed true to her husband, and was with him when he died from lung cancer, on February 15 1965. Having smoked three packs of Kool menthol cigarettes a day, Nat had been convinced that smoking had kept his voice in good trim.

LEFT
Nat King Cole with his Jazz Orchestra, 1950.

BELOW
Nat King Cole pictured in the 1950s.

PERRY
COMO

Birth name: Pierino Ronald Como
Born: May 18 1912, Canonsburg, Pennsylvania
Died: May 12 2001, Jupiter Inlet Colony, Florida
Years active: 1933 to 1994
Record label(s): Decca, RCA Victor

O ne of the most successful performers of the twentieth century, with 27 of his records going gold and 14 number one hits, Perry Como sold more than 100 million records in a career spanning over 60 years.

Perry was born the middle child of 13 to immigrant parents from Palena, Italy. His father Pietro Como, a mill worker, and his mother Lucia Travaglini Como strove to bring up their extensive brood. Perry helped the family finances by working after school, for a few cents each day, in a local barber's shop. This fired his ambition to open his own barber's shop, an ideal establishment for airing his vocal talents, after leaving high school. Singing engagements at local weddings and other events followed, the fees received helping to pay for music lessons on the baritone horn and organ. Somewhat a rarity for his time, Como's ability to read music stood him in good stead.

In 1933, while on vacation in Cleveland, Ohio, Perry was hired to sing with the Freddie Carlone band for the princely sum of $25 a week. The salary was put to good use when he married his sweetheart from high school, Roselle Belline, the daughter of a French immigrant family. Unlike many of his contemporaries, Como's marriage was an enduring partnership that lasted until the death of Roselle, in August 1998, the year of their 65th wedding anniversary. An intensely private family, they brought up their three children away from the glare of the show business spotlight.

After becoming vocalist with the Ted Weems orchestra, Perry's popularity increased such that, when the Weems orchestra disbanded in the early 1940s, he was offered a contract by NBC to share star billing with Jo Stafford on their Chesterfield Supper Club weeknight radio show. This show was televised later in the 1940s, and the exposure revealed Como's modest and captivating personality to the viewing public. A makeover, that exchanged his usual attire of a business suit for the more casual cardigan, complemented his homely, relaxed style. A brief flirtation as a movie actor, in which he made three films, *Something for the Boys* (1944), *Doll Face* (1945) and *If I'm Lucky* (1946), with co-star Carmen Miranda, led the honest Como to admit, "I was wasting their time, and they were wasting mine."

His television shows were a different matter; his friendly persona and light baritone voice endeared him to his audiences in a series that lasted for many years, a five-year contract with CBS, in 1950, being followed by eight years with NBC. His Christmas specials for ABC-TV became an integral part of the American holidays until the late 1980s. His recordings ranged from sublime ballads, including the hit that reflected his personal life in

CROONER *Legends*

its title, "No Other Love," and, the atmospheric, "Its Impossible," to the ridiculous novelty songs, "Hot Diggity Dog Ziggity Boom," and "How Much Is That Doggy In The Window?" He even made a rock-and-roll record, "Juke Box Baby," but his legacy was in the number of tuneful ballads that he recorded in his laid-back style. Perry Como has taken his place in musical history as the first vocalist to have made 10 records that each sold over one million copies. His wartime musical achievements were recognised in the 1946 award by *Billboard* magazine, as being the top-selling male singer. In 1958, the Recording Industry Association of America formally certified Como's hit single record, "Catch a Falling Star," as its first ever Gold Record. His last Top 40 hit was a cover version of the Don Maclean song, "And I Love You So", recorded in 1973 and nominated for a Grammy award that same year.

His self-deprecating manner tended to make him play down his achievements. Sales of millions of records seemed of little consequence to him, as he continually strove for perfection in his life's work, be it in the recording studio or on his television shows. He once said, "People have always thought that I wasn't ambitious. They judged by appearances and were fooled. I was competitive. I wanted success and was willing to work for it." This was summed up in New Statesman, after his death in 2001, by a critic who wrote, "Nobody else was so intensely relaxed."

Perry Como spent the later years of his life with his lifelong sweetheart Roselle, at their home in Jupiter Inlet Colony, Florida, playing golf, fishing, and going for walks with his wife. His tireless work for charity fundraising, on golf days and on radio shows, continued until the combination of old age and ill health brought an end to his activities. After his death, the Washington Post tribute included the words, "What Perry Como did week after week on his TV shows was not so much as sing to his fans as to have a continuing conversation with them, a conversation in song."

CROONER *Legends*

HARRY
CONNICKJR

Birth name: Joseph Harry Fowler Connick
Born: September 11 1967, New Orleans, Louisiana
Years active: 1980s – present
Record label(s): Columbia Records

With a number of major career successes that have brought recognition from across all branches of show business, including several platinum and gold records, Grammy, Tony, and Emmy awards, and nominations for an Oscar and a Golden Globe, Harry Connick Jr has established himself as one of America's greatest entertainers.

Born in New Orleans on September 11 1967, as Joseph Harry Fowler Connick, young Harry was fortunate to be born in a city with a great musical heritage. His parents were both successful in the legal profession: his Irish Catholic father, Harry Connick Sr, became the district attorney of New Orleans between 1977 and 2003; his mother Anita, from a New York Jewish family, became a justice in the Louisiana Supreme Court. Both parents loved music, and owned a record store. His mother used to sing to Harry when he was young, stimulating his interest in music from an early age.

A precocious musician, Harry learned to play the piano by the age of three, made his first public performance when he was six, and recorded an album, *Dixieland Plus*, with a local jazz band at the age of 10. With jazz clubs often staying open late at night, his father used to drive him to the venue, late in the evening, and collect him in the small hours of the morning. His musical talent was further developed at the New Orleans Center for the Creative Arts. After high school, Harry went to study at the City University of New York, and continued his musical education at the Manhattan School of Music. While at music school, he signed his recording contract with Columbia Records.

His first recording for Columbia was an album of instrumental standards entitled *Harry Connick Jr*. Playing in jazz clubs, and other New York showcases, further served to enhance Connick's reputation. His second album was released in November 1988 with the simple title *20*, his age at the time of recording. The album featured his vocal talent with performances of songs such as, "Blue Skies," "Lazy River," and "S'Wonderful."

His reputation became such that movie director, Rob Reiner, asked Harry to provide the soundtrack for his 1989 romantic comedy film, *When Harry Met Sally*. This he did, and the soundtrack album, featuring standards like, "It Had To be You," "Don't Get Around Much Anymore," and "Let's Call the Whole Thing Off," was a major seller, achieving double-platinum status in the US. He also won his first *Grammy* for Best Jazz Male Vocal Performance for his work on the film.

The dawning of his film-acting career came in 1990, when Harry appeared in the World War 2 drama *Memphis Belle*, in which he played a crewman in a B-17 bomber. His part in

CROONER *Legends*

CROONER *Legends*

Little Man Tate, in 1991, directed by Jodie Foster, was followed in 1995 with a convincing appearance as a homicidal killer in *Copycat*. His place in movies was cemented the following year, when he appeared alongside Will Smith in the blockbuster film, *Independence Day*.

Connick released two albums in 1990; a jazz album, *Lofty's Roach Soufflé*, and an album of standards, *We Are in Love*, which won double-platinum, and brought his second *Grammy* for Best Jazz Male Vocal. He also set out on a two-year world tour. Further multi-platinum success came in 1991, with his self-penned album *Blue Light, Red Light*. A solo piano album, *25*, also won platinum in the following year.

In December 1992, Harry was arrested at JFK airport, New York, when he was found to be in possession of a 9mm pistol. After spending a day in jail, he was given a conditional discharge, and made a television commercial warning viewers not to break firearm laws.

He married a Texan model, Jill Goodacre, in 1994, with whom he has three daughters. That year saw a temporary change in his musical direction that was not popular with all of his fans, with Harry releasing an album of New Orleans 'funk' music: it won a platinum award. He toured the UK and China, where his show was televised. The next 10 years brought more movie roles, a big band music album, *Come By Me*, in 1999, and a world tour. He wrote the score for the Broadway musical *Thou Shalt Not*, for which he received a Tony award. An ABC network television broadcast of *South Pacific*, co-starring Glen Close, and a gold record Christmas album, *Harry for the Holidays*, added to his growing list of achievements.

Harry is personally involved in the rebuilding plans for the victims of Hurricane Katrina that devastated his native city, and is honorary chair of the charity, Operation Home Delivery. It is planned to build new homes for the displaced former residents, and an arts and music centre, to be named after his tutor at the Center for the Creative Arts, Ellis Marsalis.

LEFT
Harry Connick Jr performs during the 2002 Winter Olympics Closing Ceremony.

BELOW
The versatile and talented Harry Connick Jr in 2001.

CROONER *Legends*

BING
CROSBY

Birth name: Harry Lillis Crosby
Born: May 3 1903, Tacoma, Washington
Died: October 14 1977, La Morajela golf course, near Madrid, Spain
Years active: 1920s – 1960s
Record label(s): Brunswick, Decca, Reprise, RCA Victor, Verve, United Artists

Considered by many to have been among the most talented singers of his generation, Bing Crosby was also one of the biggest selling recording artists of all time. With total record sales estimated at between 500 million and 900 million, and over 360 records in the charts of which 38 reached the No 1 position, his popularity, as a recording artist, is unquestionable. A successful radio and film career, and a business acumen that earned substantial returns on his investments made Bing a very wealthy man. However, there was a dark side to his personality.

Harry Lillis Crosby was born in Tacoma, Washington State, on May 3 1903, the fourth of seven children. His Anglo-American father, Harry Lowe Crosby, and his Irish-American mother, Catherine Harrigan Crosby, moved the family to Spokane, Washington, to seek work, in 1906. The name 'Bing' is believed to have been a contraction of the nickname Bingo, given to him at the age of six by a neighbour, after a character in a newspaper feature article.

At 17, a summer job in a Spokane theatre gave him the opportunity to see great acts, including the legendary Al Jolson. In 1920, Bing went to Gonzaga College, in Spokane, to study law. While at college he bought a drum-set and later joined a college band. The band made money, so Bing dropped his studies to follow a musical career. When the band broke up, Crosby headed for Los Angeles where, together with the former bandleader Al Rinker, they got singing jobs in movie theatres. The duo had already made their first recording "I've Got The Girl," when bandleader Paul Whiteman signed them, in 1926, to sing with his band. They were later fired after adverse audience reaction in New York, so Bing, Al and Harry Barris formed the Rhythm Boys, with Bing soon becoming front man.

Mack Sennett signed Bing for the musical, *I Surrender Dear*. Another five movies led to the break-up of the trio, so Crosby went solo. In the 1930s, Bing's career took off, not only in records, but also on the radio and in films, of which he made 79 in all. His popularity grew during World War 2, starting with his biggest hit record, "White Christmas," from the 1941 film, *Holiday Inn*. It has sold over 100 million copies world-wide: this total still rising. Crosby performed for US troops in Europe, and made propaganda broadcasts in German, earning him the nickname 'Der Bingle' from his German listeners. An Academy Award for Best Actor, in the film *Going My Way* in 1944, followed by many more film successes in the *'Road…'* series with Bob Hope, complemented his recording and radio achievements, culminating in a *Grammy* Lifetime Achievement Award in 1962.

CROONER *Legends*

CROONER *Legends*

Bing Crosby played a major role in the introduction of recording tape, to replace the metallic discs that had hitherto been used for editing and broadcasting recorded programmes. In order to help perfect his radio shows, Bing invested $50,000 of his own money in the Ampex company to further the development of magnetic tape technology that would both facilitate programme editing and allow longer recordings to be made. These improvements would reduce programme-recording time that Bing could better use to pursue his golf and horseracing interests.

Crosby was twice married: his first wife, actress/singer Dixie Lee, whom he married in 1930, bore him four sons. Dixie, an alcoholic for many years, died from ovarian cancer in 1952. Bing's second marriage in 1957, to actress Kathryn Grant, 30 years his junior, brought two more sons and a daughter. Rumours, later confirmed in a book by Gary, his son from the first marriage, had Crosby accused of meanness, child beating, and psychological abuse. Bob Hope often referred to Bing's parsimonious nature, publicly. Crosby's strange attitude towards his children from the first marriage was shown in his legacy to his four sons. His will stipulated that, apart from a small allowance, they would not receive their trust fund inheritance until they were in their eighties; none survived long enough to collect, two of his sons having committed suicide after battling alcoholism and failed careers. At his death, Bing Crosby's wealth was estimated at over $150 million.

LEFT
Bing Crosby in the recording studio, 1945.

BELOW
Bing Crosby in western pose, 1945.

His youngest son, Nathaniel Crosby, was a top amateur golfer and the youngest winner, aged 19, of the US Amateur Championship in 1981. Bing's love of sport was reflected in his part-ownership of the Pittsburgh Pirates baseball team, from 1946 to the mid-1960s, and part-ownership of horses and racing stables in California and Argentina. Bing sold his horseracing assets in 1953, to pay off taxes owed by his first wife's estate.

Bing died on the golf course at La Morajela, near Madrid, Spain, from a massive heart attack after completing 18 holes: previous medical advice from his doctor had warned him to play only nine in future.

CROONER *Legends*

VIC
DAMONE

Birth name: Vito Rocco Farinola
Born: June 12 1928, Brooklyn, New York
Years active: Late-1940s – 1990s
Record label(s): Mercury, Columbia, Capitol, RCA

Having parents with an interest in music is a decided advantage to an aspiring singer. Vic Damone was no exception. His electrician father, Rocco, both sang and played guitar, and his mother Mamie was a piano teacher. This background could not have been a more fortuitous one for the young Vito Rocco Farinola, who was born in the Brooklyn district of New York on June 12 1928. At a very early age he began to mimic his favourite singer, Frank Sinatra, and also took singing lessons and voice coaching.

His father was injured at work while the young Vic was still in his teens. With no other means of supporting the family, Vic had to drop out of school and seek paid work. He found employment as an usher and lift operator in the Paramount Theatre in Manhattan. While at the theatre, he performed for Perry Como in the star's dressing room. Como liked what he had heard and referred Vic to a local bandleader, in order that he could gain experience as a performer. It was around this time that he took his mother's surname, Damone, for his stage name.

In April 1947, Damone entered the competition to find new talent on the weekly radio show *Arthur Godfrey's Talent Scouts*, which he duly won, earning himself the prize of a regular spot on that show. *Talent Scouts* was renowned over the years for showcasing artists such as Tony Bennett, Eddie Fisher, Steve Lawrence and Al Martino. Other notables who auditioned for the show, but were not chosen to appear, were Buddy Holly and Elvis Presley. At the radio station he met the actor and comedian Milton Berle, who had a vast range of show business contacts: using these led to Berle finding some regular appearances at two New York night-clubs for Damone. By the summer of 1947, Vic was given a recording contract with Mercury Records.

His first two releases for Mercury, "I Have But One Heart" and "You Do," were released in 1947 and both achieved the No 7 placing on the *Billboard* charts. More hit records followed, leading to Vic being given his own weekly radio show in 1948, *Saturday Night Serenade*. By 1951, the movies had beckoned, with Vic making two films that year for MGM, a drama starring Mickey Rooney, *The Strip*, in which Vic played himself, and the musical *Rich, Young and Pretty* opposite Jane Powell. This musical was the first of several made by Damone for MGM that include *Athena* (1953), *Deep In My Heart* (1954) and, perhaps the best of the bunch, *Kismet* (1955).

A prolific recording artist, 39 of his releases made the *Billboard* charts, with two of them, "Again" and "You're Breaking My Heart" (both in 1949) winning him gold records. His

CROONER *Legends*

LEFT
Vic Damone and Liza
Minnelli in rehearsal.

baritone voice was used to good effect on a range of romantic ballads from musical films including *Gigi*, and also on the more upbeat songs "Tzena, Tzena, Tzena" and "My Truly, Truly Fair."

With the prospect of two years in the US Army from 1951-53 on the horizon, Vic recorded a number of songs that were released while he served Uncle Sam. After military duty, he married the actress Pier Angeli in 1954, a short-lived union that was dissolved in 1958. Apart from the film *Kismet*, his career took a downward slide in 1955, with his only record placement in the charts, "Por Favor," reaching No 73. Early in the following year he lost his contract with Mercury, then was signed by Columbia for whom he had the hits "On the Street Where You Live" (from *My Fair Lady*), and the title song from the film *An Affair To Remember*.

A series of guest host appearances on television shows kept Vic in the public eye for a few years but, in 1960, he made what was to be his last feature film, *Hell To Eternity,* a wartime action drama about a heroic US marine. A year later, he was released by Columbia Records and joined Capitol, who had lost Frank Sinatra when he left to be one of the founders of the Reprise label. Leaving Capitol, where he had made some of his best albums, he moved to the Warner Brothers label in 1965. There he had one chart success, "You Were Only Fooling (While I Was Falling In Love)," before moving labels again, this time to RCA, where he released his last record for more than 20 years.

Beset by bankruptcy in the early 1970s, Damone sang in Las Vegas, and toured both the US and the UK to help restore his financial status. He married his current wife, fashion designer Rena Rowan in 1992. Many of Vic's recent compilation albums have sold well, and have brought the work of this fine singer to the attention of a new generation of music lovers.

CROONER *Legends*

SAMMY
DAVIS JR

Birth name: Samuel George Davis, Jr
Born: December 8 1925, Harlem, New York
Died: May 16 1990, Beverly Hills, California
Years active: 1930s – 1980s
Record label(s): Brunswick, Decca, Capitol, Reprise, Motown, United Artists

From his early years in vaudeville, to the casino theatres of Las Vegas, the career of Sammy Davis, Jr ranged from song-and-dance man, Broadway show performer, film actor, recording star and cabaret artist. At times a controversial personality, he was a political activist who made a major impact in the struggle against racism in the US, as he played a prominent role in the civil rights movement.

Samuel George Davis, Jr was born in the Harlem district of New York on December 8 1925. His father, Sammy Davis, Sr was an African-American vaudeville entertainer, as was his mother, Elvera Sanchez, a Cuban-American. His parents were often on the road so his grandmother brought up Sammy. At the age of three, Sammy's parents separated; his father, anxious not to lose custody, took the youngster with him on tour. There, he learned to dance with his father and the man he called 'uncle', Will Mastin, and soon, when still a child, became a member of the Will Mastin Trio, forging a lifelong bond between them. This bond existed to the extent that, even after Sammy Jr had gone solo, he still gave the trio billing on his show, and paid his father and Will a generous percentage of his earnings.

The two older men both played a large part in protecting the young Sammy from the overt racism that existed in the US at the time. It came as a great shock to him when, while serving in the US Army during World War 2, Sammy Jr came into first-hand contact with racial prejudice. He later used his talent as an army entertainer to deflect some of the racist hatred, hoping to bridge the void between cultural differences. After the war he rejoined the trio, as well as working on his solo career. In 1949, he recorded his first of many albums and singles. His treatment of songs from the shows later earned him a major role in Mr Wonderful on Broadway in 1956.

A car crash in 1954 left him without his left eye. In hospital, he learned of the similarities between the Jewish and Black cultures, and the intolerance both races had suffered, from his friend Eddie Cantor. Sammy converted to Judaism around this time. His inner strength and resolve against racism was put to the test when, in 1960, he married the white Swedish actress, May Britt. Sammy endured threats against his life from white extremist groups, leading to the early closure of his *Tony*-nominated performance in the Broadway musical, *Golden Boy*, in the mid-1960s. An admitted affair with singer Lola Falana, one of many women in his life, led to divorce in 1968. In the same year, he began dating a dancer from the show *Golden Boy*, Altovise Gore, who he married in 1970, the wedding ceremony being conducted by the Reverend Jesse Jackson.

CROONER *Legends*

Davis joined the fight against prejudice that allowed black people to perform in hotels and casinos in Las Vegas, but not to rent rooms there. As his star status grew, Sammy and other top black performers refused to appear at venues where racial segregation existed, resulting in the eventual integration of premises in both Miami Beach and Las Vegas.

In 1959, Davis became a member of the group originally known as 'The Clan' led by his friend Frank Sinatra. Sammy objected to the name 'Clan', with its racist connotation, so it became 'The Summit', but was more commonly known as the 'Rat Pack'. His association brought accusations and innuendo suggesting that Sammy had Mafia connections, along with some of his fellow members.

Sammy Davis, Jr was a tireless workaholic, often putting his acting, television and recording work before family obligations. A long-time heavy drinker, he gradually became addicted to cocaine. His use of drugs caused him to be shunned by his friend Sinatra, who despised narcotic users. They were reconciled after Sammy gave up drugs: however, he remained a chain-smoker, which had earned him his Rat Pack sobriquet, Smokey; it would eventually cost him his life.

In 1961, although a confirmed Democratic voter, Davis felt snubbed by the White House, after being removed from the list of performers at JF Kennedy's inauguration celebrations. He believed this was because of his inter-racial marriage, a political thorn in the side of the US ruling party. Within 10 years, Sammy was wholeheartedly supporting the Republican candidate, Richard Nixon, and was widely criticised for it within the black community.

Davis worked in cabaret, television, and recorded for Motown during the 70s and 80s. His death from throat cancer, in 1990, left his widow Altovise with the task of selling off much of his memorabilia to settle his estate that owed over $7.5 million in unpaid taxes. Over 10 years after his death, he was given a *Grammy* Lifetime Achievement Award.

CROONER *Legends*

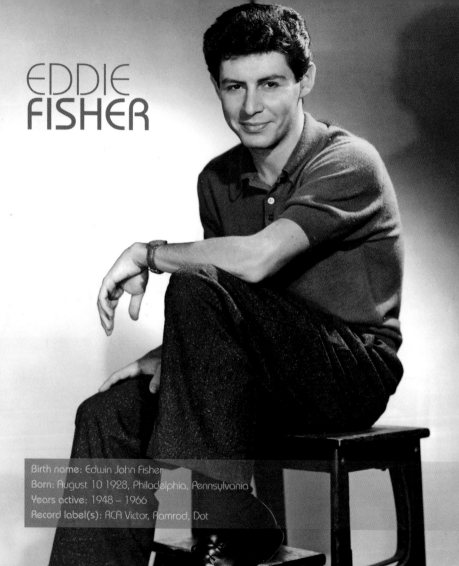

EDDIE
FISHER

Birth name: Edwin John Fisher
Born: August 10 1928, Philadelphia, Pennsylvania
Years active: 1948 – 1966
Record label(s): RCA Victor, Ramrod, Dot

During the 1950s, Eddie Fisher was, along with Perry Como and Elvis Presley, one of RCA Victor's top three best-selling recording stars. His comparatively short career was carried out in the spotlight of public attention, famous not only for his singing but also his high-profile matrimonial affairs, alcoholism, drug addiction and gambling. With candid honesty, he never shied away from admitting to his personal failings although, according to his autobiography, some of his wives were not entirely free from blame, either.

Edwin John Fisher was born in the City of Brotherly Love, Philadelphia, on August 10 1928 to Joseph and Kate Fisher, the fourth of their seven children. His parents were of Russian-Jewish origin where their surname was believed to have originally been 'Fisch', but became Fisher during the immigration process. The young Eddie was known within the family circle as Sonny Boy. Still very young when his talent as a singer became apparent, he was soon entering, and often winning, amateur talent contests.

While at high school, he performed on a local radio show, then later appeared on the network radio talent show that had unearthed many well-known entertainers in the 1940s, *Arthur Godfrey's Talent Scouts.* By the age of 18, Fisher was crooning with the big-name bands of Buddy Morrow and Charlie Ventura. His career took off when, at the age of 21, he was spotted by Eddie Cantor, who gave him exposure on Cantor's nationally networked radio programme. He was an immediate hit, and was soon rewarded with a recording contract by RCA Victor.

Called up for service with the US Army in 1951, Eddie spent a year in Korea before being drafted into the US Army Chorus, in Washington DC. Although conscripted, patriotic publicity pictures of him wearing army uniform gave his career a boost after demobilisation. He was given star billing as a singer in top night-clubs and, within the next four years, had two television series of his own, as well as making guest appearances on others.

His recording career was a great success, with Eddie becoming one of the most popular singers of the 1950s. In the first six years of that decade, he had 17 records in the Top 10 charts and 35, in total, that made the Top 40. Three reached the coveted No 1 position, "Wish You Were Here" (1952), "Oh My Pa-Pa," a million-seller in 1953, and a duet with Sally Sweetland also in 1953, "I'm Walking Behind You." His television achievements brought him a Golden Globe award in 1957.

An idol of American teenagers, especially the girls, he made his film debut, starring with his wife Debbie Reynolds, whom he had married late in 1955, in the 1956 musical

CROONER *Legends*

comedy *Bundle of Joy*. He also played a serious role in *Butterfield 8*, in which his then wife Elizabeth Taylor was the female lead.

His great friend, producer and entrepreneur Mike Todd, who was the husband of Elizabeth Taylor, was killed in a plane crash in 1958. Fisher's subsequent affair with Todd's widow caused a major Hollywood scandal that led to a messy and very public divorce from Debbie in 1959, leaving him free to marry Taylor that same year. This marriage lasted until 1965, and was followed by a two-year marriage to actress Connie Stevens from 1967-69. An even shorter marriage to Terry Richard in 1975 ended in divorce the following year. He was married for the fifth time in 1993 to Betty Lin, the union lasting until her death from cancer in 2001. Fisher has admitted affairs with many other women, and has documented these in his second autobiography, published in 1981, *Eddie: My Life, My Loves*.

After his career as a recording artist stalled in the late 1950s, Eddie released his live recorded album, *Eddie Fisher at the Winter Garden*, on his own label Ramrod. He rejoined RCA in the mid-1960s and made three albums, *Games That Lovers Play, People Like You* and *You Ain't Heard Nothin' Yet*. In 1965, his album release on the Dot label, *Eddie Fisher Today*, reached only No 72 on the album charts, with a mixture of standards and songs from the shows. Three more albums, *When I Was Young, Mary Christmas,* and *Young and Foolish*, were also released in 1965 on the Dot label, and a greatest hits album in 1968. Although not chart-toppers, these releases brought in a few more dollars but effectively signalled the end of Fisher as a recording artist.

LEFT
Eddie Fisher in the recording studio.

BELOW
Publicity shot of Eddie Fisher at the height of his fame.

Towards the end of his performing career, he made few recordings but continued to sing at venues around the US, including top-ranking concert halls and Las Vegas hotel and casino show theatres. His two stars on the Hollywood Walk of Fame, one for his recordings, the other recognising his television work, tell of his career achievements.

ENGELBERT
HUMPERDINCK

Birth name: Arnold George Dorsey
Born: May 2 1936, Madras, India
Years active: Early-1950s – present
Record label(s): Decca, Mercury, London, Epic, Columbia, Varesse, Image

I n over 40 years at the top of the entertainment business, one man has defined the world of romance in song, having sold more than 130 million records, including 64 gold and 24 platinum albums. With a stage name that was originally a publicity-seeking gimmick, Engelbert Humperdinck has become one of the world's greatest entertainers. His voice, coupled with his warm personality and great sense of humour, has endeared him to his millions of fans from all over the world.

Arnold George Dorsey was born in Madras, India, on May 2 1936, the youngest boy of three and seven girls. His father was serving in the British forces and had met his Indian-born wife while serving on the sub-continent. The family moved to England in 1946 and settled in the Leicester area. The young Arnold became interested in music and, at the age of 11 years, began to study the saxophone. In his mid-teens, while playing saxophone at a pub talent contest his friends, who knew of his talent for mimicry, persuaded him to enter the show with his vocal impression of Jerry Lewis. He soon acquired the name Gerry as his stage name, and started singing in night-clubs until military service placed his professional career on hold for two years.

Back in civilian life in 1958, he was signed by Decca but his only single release, "I'll Never Fall in Love Again," failed to sell. Dorsey continued performing until 1961, when he was stricken with tuberculosis that could have ended his career and possibly, his life. In 1965, a meeting with an old roommate, promoter and manager Gordon Mills, was to have an impact on his future career, as well as bringing another change of name. The astute Mills realised that, in order to make the grade in the music industry against the highly competitive rock music groups of the day, a stage name that was both distinctive and unforgettable was needed. He first persuaded Dorsey that the name of the German composer, Engelbert Humperdinck, would fit both requirements, and also secured a record deal with Decca.

In 1967, his recording of "Release Me" achieved a major success for Engelbert, rapidly reaching the No 1 position in the British charts, selling up to 85,000 copies daily, and famously beating the Beatles' "Strawberry Fields Forever" to that spot. Similar success followed in the American charts, firmly imprinting the name of Humperdinck in the minds of the record-buying public, particularly those of the female gender. His career took off in the late 1960s and early 70s, selling millions of records of love songs, and starring in stage shows at the rate of around 100 performances in a year. At one time, his fan club

was claimed to have the largest membership of any similar organisation in the world, over eight million, all potential record buyers and every one of them eager for Engelbert's next record release.

In the 1970s, as popular music moved into another style, his records began to sell less well than previously so Engelbert put more of his energies into his stage shows. These became more lavish and spectacular, ideally suited to the casino theatres of Las Vegas and elsewhere. His honesty and loyalty to his fans were demonstrated by his desire to give them something different from anything they might have seen before, and he has been quoted as saying, "I take the job description of 'entertainer' very seriously!"

His 1976 album, *After the Lovin'*, earned him the critical acclaim he deserved, a *Grammy* Award being his first major honour granted by the show business industry. Engelbert had been given little artistic control over his album recordings until late in the 1980s but after that time his output took on a wider appeal, although love songs still featured largely in his chosen musical content. By 1980, just a few years short of his 50th birthday, he was still making albums, performing in over 200 concerts each year, and was still a major attraction for his female fans. Through all this, he managed to maintain a close family life with his wife, Patricia, and their four children. The children are all involved in the 'family business' and the family travels frequently between their homes in Leicestershire and Beverly Hills, California.

In 1989, further honours came Humperdinck's way when he was given a star on the Hollywood Walk of Fame and a Golden Globe Award for Entertainer of the Year. Around this time, he began a continuing major involvement with charity organisations, both in Britain and the US. Still keeping up a punishing schedule in his 70s, the man with the pretentious-sounding name has been described as "… a true gentleman." His recording of "Jerusalem" was selected as the England anthem for the Rugby World Cup 2007, a song that will help to keep Engelbert Humperdinck's name in the forefront of public awareness.

LEFT
Engelbert has always had a way with the ladies.

BELOW
Engelbert Humperdinck pictured in 2004.

JACK JONES

Birth name: John Allan Jones

Born: January 14 1938, Hollywood, California

Years active: 1957 – mid-2000s

Record label(s): Capitol, Kapp Records (London, in the UK), RCA, MGM, Sony/Legacy, Honest Entertainment

W ith musical influences from artistes such as Frank Sinatra, Tony Bennett and Mel Tormé, together with a singing talent inherited from his father, it is no wonder that Jack Jones went on to record over 50 albums, of which 17 reached the Billboard Top 20. With two Grammys for his singles, "Lollipops and Roses" and "Wives and Lovers", both public and music industry alike have recognised the vocal achievements of this great singer.

The son of singer and movie actor Allan Jones and popular actress Irene Hervey, Jack was born on the same night that his father had recorded his best-known hit, "Donkey Serenade". Jack's formative years were spent as a privileged but talented scholar, first at junior school, then at University High School in Los Angeles. Although he played down his show business background, while at high school he studied drama and took private singing lessons paid for by his father. His talents were not limited to the performing arts: track and field athletics and football were among his accomplishments, although he later gave up his on-the-field activities to concentrate on the performing aspects of his education. At high school, an event took place that sowed the seed for Jack's future career plan. A friend and fellow pupil, Nancy Sinatra, persuaded her father to sing in the school theatre; this was the spark that lit the fire in Jack's ambition.

His life was turned topsy-turvy when his parents divorced and, on graduating from school, was faced with a harsher financial situation than he had ever been in before. He eventually made his debut on the professional stage when he was 19 years old. A small part in his father's act at the Thunderbird Hotel in Las Vegas gave Jack the incentive to start his own solo singing career, with other casual work helping to pay his way in life. After recording a demonstration record for songwriter Don Raye, he was signed by Capitol for whom he recorded several unsuccessful singles and an album. Although Jack had a low opinion of the album, one track impressed the owner of a San Francisco club, who gave him a three-week booking there. At that club, Pete King, a producer for Kapp Records heard him, and promptly signed Jones to that label.

Jack's reputation was enhanced by his ability to choose songs, and interpret them in a respectful and emotional manner, written by the great songwriters of the day including, Cole Porter, George and Ira Gershwin, and a particular favourite writer of his, Michel Legrand. In 1971, Jones paid the Frenchman Legrand a huge compliment by recording the first vocal album, in English, of the composer's songs. This album, *Jack Jones Sings Michel*

CROONER *Legends*

Legrand, is one of the singer's personal favourites. He made records that brought more awards: his version of "Wives and Lovers" was nominated for Record of the Year, as was "The Impossible Dream".

Away from the recording studio, Jack made appearances in several lesser films, such as *The Comeback* and, more recently, in the feature-length British TV comedy *Cruise of the Gods* in which he co-starred with Steve Coogan. Over a number of years, his impact on the stage in musicals such as *Guys and Dolls, South Pacific*, and *The Pajama Game* brought him acclaim from audiences and critics alike. Theme songs from films, including "The Love Boat" gave wider exposure to his vocal talents. Touring still features on Jack's schedule, having completed a series of shows across Britain during 2006. Guest appearances on television, personal appearances and charity fund-raising all keep him active after 50 years in show business. A deserved honour came Jack's way in 1989 when he was given his own star on the Hollywood Walk of Fame, close to that of his father.

A series of well-publicised affairs and failed marriages dogged this good-looking, all-American singer throughout his life until, in 1982, he married for the fifth time, to his English-born wife Kim. This marriage has stood the test of time and the pair, with their daughter Nicole, born in 1991, now reside in Palm Springs. Nicole has appeared on stage with her father, during her school holidays, and also in her own right in local productions in Palm Springs. One of Jack's greatest friendships has been with Tony Bennett, who he met at Bennett's last night of a season at a Chicago hotel in 1960, with Jones taking over the residency from his new friend the following day. In 1998, in celebration of their friendship, Jack released a tribute album, *Jack Jones Paints A Tribute to Tony Bennett*, sung in the distinctive and stylish Jones manner. Frank Sinatra once said of Jones, "Jack is one of the major singers of our time," and Mel Tormé called him, "...the greatest 'pure' singer in the world."

LEFT
Jack Jones with actress Loni Anderson, 2003.

STEVE LAWRENCE

Birth name: Sidney Leibowitz

Born: July 8 1935, Brooklyn, New York

Years active: 1950s to mid-2000s

Record label(s): King, Coral, ABC-Paramount, United Artists, Calendar, Columbia, RCA Victor, MGM Records, Applause Records, GL Music (Gorme/Lawrence own label)

The versatile Steve Lawrence has enjoyed a successful singing career, both as a solo artist and as part of a double act with his wife, Eydie Gorme, which has spanned over half a century. The son of a painter and part-time cantor in a synagogue, Steve was born Sidney Leibowitz in the Brownville district of Brooklyn, New York, on July 8 1935. His father Max first introduced his young son to performing in public in the synagogue. When his voice broke, Sidney gave up singing for a while, but studied music, learned to play the piano and saxophone, and also began to write and arrange songs. When his voice had stabilised, he resumed singing and took vocal coaching lessons.

He began touting his musical talents around the song publishing companies that were based in the Brill Building on Broadway, singing on demonstration records of new songs. It was around this time that he changed his name to the more marketable, Steve Lawrence. An appearance on the 1951 amateur television show, *Arthur Godfrey Talent Scouts*, netted him top prize. His first recording contract followed in 1952 when, still only 16 years old, King Records signed him. During the next two years, King released eight singles by Steve; his second release "Poinciana" made his first entry into the record sales charts in June 1952. By 1953, his first album, with the eponymous title *Steve Lawrence*, firmly established his credentials as a fine singer of ballads. In July of that year, Steve was given a spot on a local television show *Tonight!* hosted by Steve Allen, later networked by NBC.

By this time Lawrence had already moved from King to Coral Records, the first of many changes of label. While working on *Tonight!* he met another singer, Eydie Gorme, who was to become his partner on stage, and his future wife. His second release for Coral was the first recording of the pair performing as a duo, featuring the Bob Merrill song "Make Yourself Comfortable". In 1955 his second album *About That Girl*, and his third, in 1956, *Songs by Steve Lawrence*, were released by Coral. Steve continued to make records both as a solo artiste, and duets with Gorme, but chart success eluded him until late 1956, when his cover version of the Harry Belafonte song, "The Banana Boat Song" made it into the Top 20. Another cover version, this time of Buddy Knox's "Party Doll" rose to the Top 5, although the original had reached the coveted No 1 position. His hit records brought him onto the play-lists of disc jockeys across the States, charting two more singles within a year. New vistas opened for him on television shows where he made many guest appearances, notably on the *General Motors Fiftieth Anniversary Show* on November 17 1957, which was recorded on album by RCA Victor.

CROONER *Legends*

Lawrence and Gorme married in Las Vegas on December 29 1957. Six months later his fourth album, *Here's Steve Lawrence*, made the Top 20 Album Chart. An eight-week networked TV show, *Steve Allen Presents the Steve Lawrence and Eydie Gorme Show*, followed in the summer of 1957. The US Army was next to call on Steve's services; his two-year stint from the age of 23 was served as a singer with an Army band. Allowed to continue his recording career while serving, he made his fifth and final LP for Coral, *All About Love*, before joining the ABC-Paramount label in early 1959. His third and fourth singles for the new company, "Pretty Blue Eyes" and "Footsteps" both reached the Top 10. His sixth album *Swing Softly With Me* soon followed.

After leaving the Army, he and Eydie continued their careers as a duo. Although Steve made many more singles, and two more albums, it was 1961 before he made the charts with "Portrait of My Love", earning him a *Grammy* nomination for Best Vocal Performance. Thirty of his records made the *BillBoard* Easy Listening Chart. His most successful year in record sales was in 1963 with his gold disc No 1 seller, "Go Away Little Girl". A succession of solo hits and a couple of duets with Eydie were followed by a career move that minimised the impact of the rock era on the charts. A part in a smash hit Broadway musical that ran for 540 performances in 1965, and another in 1967 that ran for 385 showings, preceded a TV and club partnership with Eydie that lasted into the 21st century. Notable events included a 10-year show-time spot at Caesar's Palace, Las Vegas, and as the opening act in Frank Sinatra's Diamond Jubilee Tour in 1990-91, during which Frank befriended Steve and later gave him his book of arrangements when Frank retired. Lawrence used the arrangements to make his tribute album *Steve Lawrence Sings Sinatra* for his own GL Music label in 2003.

LEFT
Steve Lawrence shares a joke with Jerry Lewis on stage in 2004.

BELOW
Steve Lawrence performs with Eydie Gorme, 1967.

BARRY
MANILOW

Birth name: Barry Alan Pincus
Born: June 17 1943, Brooklyn, New York
Years active: 1970s – present
Record label(s): Bell (later Arista), RCA Records, Concord

Barry Manilow has often been derided by his critics as a 'pop singer' and flamboyant showman but has, nevertheless, endeared himself to his many, largely female, fans. His musical pedigree is without question, as a writer, arranger and musical director, and as a singer of swing tunes, jazz, and evergreen ballads.

Barry Alan Pincus was born on June 17 1943. When he was only two years old, his father, Harold Pincus, left the family, so his mother Edna and Barry went to live with his Russian-Jewish maternal grandparents, Joseph and Esther Manilow. Barry made his first recording in 1948, at the age of 5 years, when he sang "Happy Birthday" that was made into a 78rpm record for his grandfather, as a gift for a family member. Barry has twice used samples from this recording in albums recorded in the 1970s.

His interest in music developed when he started to play the accordion, a popular instrument around his Italian/Jewish neighbourhood, in the early 50s. When he was 13, in the year of his Bar Mitzvah, his stepfather gave him a piano as a birthday present. His mother also legally changed his surname to Manilow that same year. In the five years before he graduated from high school, he established himself as 'the' local pianist. With his eyes firmly set on achieving musical celebrity, emulating his idols, Harold Arlen, Irving Berlin and Cole Porter, Barry took a course of study at the Juilliard College of Music, New York, paying his fees with earnings from working in the post room at CBS Broadcasting.

Barry later gained employment at CBS as a musical director of the show Callback and also wrote, produced and performed radio-advertising jingles for companies like Dr Pepper, McDonalds and Kentucky Fried Chicken. He also wrote a musical score for a melodrama, *The Drunkard*, which ran for eight years. In 1964, Manilow married his sweetheart from high school, Susan Deixler, but the marriage ended in 1966, when Barry asked for a divorce.

In 1971, Bette Midler hired him as her pianist, arranger and musical director and, in the following year, was given a spot on her Carnegie Hall show, where he performed some of his own material. This led to a recording contract with the new Bell label, for which he released his less than successful debut album, *Barry Manilow 1*, in 1973. When Bell was taken over by Arista, the company asked him to record a version of "Brandy", a song that had been a hit in England for its co-writer Scott English. Manilow changed it from a pop song to a ballad, renamed it "Mandy" and, after releasing it on his 1974 album *Barry Manilow II*, it became a No 1 hit early in the next year.

CROONER *Legends*

His next release hit the Top 20, followed by a Top 10 appearance with "Could It Be Magic", a single from his first album. The late 70s became Manilow's most fruitful period in record sales with his second No 1 hit, "I Write The Songs" (1976), a triple platinum album, *This One's for You*, in the same year, followed by another No 1 in 1977, "Looks Like We Made It". After several further successes, the momentum gradually slowed following his last Top 10 placement, "I Made It Through The Rain".

Although he frequented the charts on many occasions in the next few years, in 1984 Barry took a change in career direction towards jazz and swing music, with albums like *Swing Street* (1987), *Singin' With The Big Bands* (1994) and Manilow *Sings Sinatra* (1998). He also wrote and performed the stage musicals *Copacabana* (1994) and *Harmony* (1999).

A change in record company to Concord, a jazz label, in 2001, heralded a return to his more popular music style. At the 2002 pre-game show for the US Super Bowl, Manilow performed a new song, "Let Freedom Ring", which brought him back into public focus as a recording artist. In March of that year, his new album, *Ultimate Manilow*, entered the album charts at No 3. A DVD of his collection was followed by a two-CD album of live performances called *2 Nights Live*. The former head of Arista, Clive Davis, produced a 2005 studio album featuring Barry singing tracks from the 1950s, called *Greatest Songs of the Fifties* that went to the top of the album charts in 2006. The latter part of 2006 saw a companion release, *Greatest Songs of the Sixties*.

After a recent 'farewell' tour, Manilow showed both his great sense of humour and self-deprecation when he said, "It must have been another generation that discovered me. Or maybe they were brainwashed by their parents and wanted to see me before I died. 'Look, he's still breathing. Buy the ticket!'"

DEAN MARTIN

Birth name: Dino Paul Crocetti
Born: June 7 1917, Steubenville, Ohio
Died: December 25 1995, Beverly Hills, Los Angeles
Years active: 1940s – late 1970s
Record label(s): Capitol, Reprise

A man who could not read music recorded more than 100 albums, had many major hit singles, and also starred in movies and television shows. He became a show business icon, yet was uncomfortable in the glare of publicity and was not overly impressed with stardom. After many years in the public eye, Dean Martin became almost reclusive in his later years, particularly after losing his son, a pilot, in an air crash.

Dino Paul Crocetti was born on June 7 1917 in Steubenville, Ohio, the son of an immigrant Italian barber, Gaetano Crocetti and his wife, Angela. Dino spoke only Italian until he went to school, aged 5 years. This caused him to suffer the taunts of his fellow schoolmates for his broken English and probably accounted for his poor reading skills, recounting in later life that he had only ever read one book, Black Beauty, preferring instead, comic books that he asked others to buy for him.

A school drop-out at 15, he was employed in diverse odd jobs, from steelworker to bootleg alcohol deliveries, and also took up prize-fighting, as 'Kid Crochet', from which activity he received a little prize money, along with a broken nose. He later gave up fighting to work in an illegal casino, as a croupier, and started to sing with local bands, billed as Dino Martini. In the early 1940s, he worked with bandleader Sammy Watkins, changing his name to Dean Martin around that time. He married his first wife, Betty McDonald, with whom he had four children before their divorce in 1949.

Dean succeeded Frank Sinatra at a club in 1943; although Dean was a flop, their meeting was the start of a long acquaintance. Martin was renowned for bad money management, mainly because he was earning so little, and often sold percentages of his future earnings for cash advances. This could have been the beginning of his alleged Mafia connections. After serving for one year in the US Army, Dean was discharged on medical grounds. By 1946, he was becoming more successful as a night-club singer, but was not as popular as Sinatra, who was a major attraction. A meeting with an up-and-coming comic at a New York club, where they were both performing, was the beginning of the, later, world famous double-act, Dean Martin and Jerry Lewis. As they built their act their audiences grew, leading to them being given a radio series in 1949, followed by a film contract with Paramount, in Hollywood.

Although their Paramount contract only netted the pair $75,000 between them, a private venture with their own company York Productions, coupled with stage, radio and television shows, and recording contracts, earned the pair millions. As part of the hottest

CROONER *Legends*

act in the US, Dean was adored by his many female fans who loved to watch as he sang romantic ballads, one of which, "That's Amore", became a hit in 1953. By 1956, Dean was growing tired of his partner's on-stage antics and jealousy so, after many months of work by lawyers, the partnership was dissolved.

Having made many comedy films with Lewis, a straight-acting role alongside Marlon Brando in *The Young Lions* in 1957 served to bring Dean's career back into the spotlight. Several more films and a series of hit records including "Memories Are Made of This", "Volare", and "You're Nobody Till Somebody Loves You" culminated in the record that became his theme song, "Everybody Loves Somebody", knocking the Beatles from No 1 position in 1964. For the next 20 years or so, Dean was one of the top draws in Las Vegas and elsewhere. His television appearances perpetuated the public's opinion of him as a laid-back half-drunk crooner, who was also a ladies man. His persona as a drinker was reflected in his car license plate, DRUNKY, although it has been said that he often drank only apple juice during his television shows.

LEFT
Dean Martin on his ranch, 1965.

BELOW
Dean Martin at the Variety Club luncheon in his honour, 1983.

His membership of the Rat Pack with Sinatra, Peter Lawford, Sammy Davis, Jr, *et al*, added to his wild-living reputation and, although he participated fully in the boozy alliance, was often first to leave the party, particularly when film or television work was on the next day's schedule. In 1965, he starred in his own NBC networked TV series, *The Dean Martin Show,* which ran for nine seasons. Many more television specials, as well as the 'Matt Helm' series of films followed this. By the late 1970s, health problems restricted Dean to the casino show stages. In 1987, his son Dean Paul Martin, a fighter pilot in the California Air National Guard, was killed in a crash; devastated by the loss, Dean never got over it, and became even more withdrawn and virtually reclusive.

Dean Martin died of respiratory failure on Christmas Day 1995. Las Vegas dimmed the lights on the Strip in homage, and named a road, Dean Martin Drive, in his memory.

CROONER *Legends*

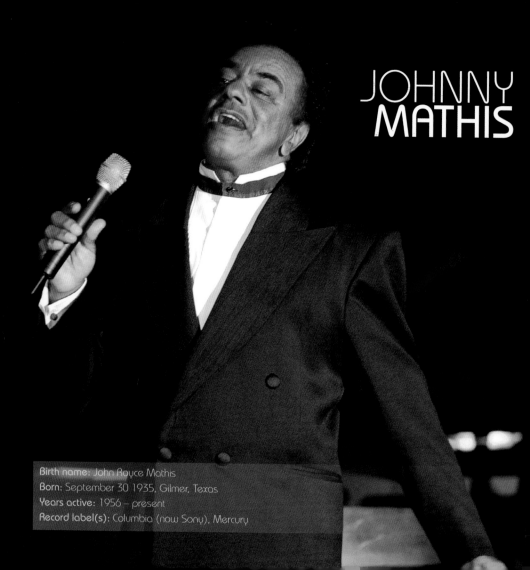

JOHNNY
MATHIS

Birth name: John Royce Mathis
Born: September 30 1935, Gilmer, Texas
Years active: 1956 – present
Record label(s): Columbia (now Sony), Mercury

Emerging into the music industry in the latter end of the 50s, Johnny Mathis was one of the last of the traditional male singers to emerge before the rock era began. With a series of popular records Mathis became the USA's third best-selling male singer, after Elvis Presley and Frank Sinatra, with over 350 million records sold. Over 60 of his albums made the Billboard charts, with over a third of these achieving the coveted gold or platinum status. He was also the first black entertainer to become a millionaire before the age of 21.

Johnny Mathis was born in Gilmer, Texas, on September 30 1935, the fourth of seven children. His parents, Clem and Mildred Mathis moved to San Francisco, California, while Johnny was young, and raised their family there. At an early age his father, a former vaudeville performer, spotted his son's talent and bought an old piano for $25, to encourage him to develop his musical education. He also taught Johnny some song and dance routines that entertained visitors to their home, eventually leading to public performances at school concerts and at church events. When Mathis was 13, his father enrolled him with a voice teacher, Connie Cox, who agreed to the arrangement that her pupil would pay for lessons by doing odd jobs around her house. For six years he studied under Connie's guidance, improving his voice projection, practising vocal scales, and learning classical operatic techniques.

At high school, Johnny became a star athlete in track and field as a hurdler and notably, a high jumper, as well as being a very competent basketball player. This led to a scholarship at San Francisco State College to study for teaching qualifications in English and Physical Education. He broke the college high jump record in 1954, with a leap of 6ft 5in. While performing at a college function, he was spotted by Helen Noga, the owner of The Black Hawk Club, who became his manager. At a weekend singing performance, his manager had brought George Avakian, a producer from Columbia Records, to hear him. Impressed by Mathis, he sent a well-documented telegram to the Columbia bosses, "Have found phenomenal 19-year-old who could go all the way. Send blank contracts." This they did, and before long, Avakian's prophecy was fulfilled.

One other major honour to come the way of Mathis was an invitation to attend for trials for the 1956 USA Olympic athletics team. Advised by his father, he travelled instead to New York to make his first recordings that were released in 1956. His first album, *Johnny Mathis: A New Sound in Popular Song*, was jazz-orientated and a slow seller. His

CROONER *Legends*

producer at Columbia, the famous Mitch Miller, steered Mathis away from jazz towards the soft, romantic ballads that were to become his hallmark. Two of his 1956 recordings, "Wonderful, Wonderful", and "It's Not For Me To Say", the latter used on the soundtrack of the film *Lizzie* in the following year, soon became classics of the genre. After appearing on the *Ed Sullivan Show,* and small parts in a couple of movies, his future stardom was assured. Mathis bought himself a mansion in the Hollywood Hills district, formerly the residence of Howard Hughes; he still lives there today. He then set up his own companies Jon Mat Records Inc, which handled his recording interests, and Rojon Productions Inc, to look after all his concert and personal appearance business. Since the death of his business manager in 1984, Johnny has managed all aspects of his own career from his offices in Burbank, California.

Apart from a three-year period in the 1960s, Mathis has remained with Columbia/Sony for his entire recording career in which he made over 350 million record sales spanning a wide variety of musical styles including jazz, Latin-American, soul, R&B and country, as well his Christmas songs. His 110 albums and over 200 singles are testament to his popularity and longevity as a recording star. His album *Johnny's Greatest Hits* stayed in the *Billboard* Album Charts for 490 consecutive weeks, or 9½ years, the *Guinness Book of Records* confirming a feat unmatched by any other performer. Only two others, Frank Sinatra and Barry Manilow have equalled his achievement of having five albums in the *Billboard* charts, simultaneously. His career, spanning six decades, has brought Mathis three *Grammy* awards and six nominations, and two Oscar nominations for soundtrack songs. He has made 12 television specials and appeared on over 300 other TV shows.

His sexuality has always been in question, having been quoted in a magazine article as saying, "Homosexuality is a way of life that I've grown accustomed to," and yet he has faced paternity claims on several occasions. A keen golfer, and an accomplished cook, Mathis has recently 'scaled down' his workload to around 50 concerts a year.

MATT
MONRO

Birth name: Terence Edward Parsons
Born: December 1 1930, Shoreditch, London
Died: February 7 1985, Cromwell Hospital, London
Years active: Mid-1950s – 1984
Record label(s): Decca, Fontana, Parlophone, Capitol, Columbia

Known as 'The Singer's Singer', many of his contemporaries admired the artistry of the man, even though they were rivals in the same business. Great stars paid compliments to his singing, one paid tribute after his death with these words, "His pitch was right on the nose: his word enunciations letter perfect: his understanding of a song thorough. He will be missed very much not only by me, but by his fans all over the world". So said the great Frank Sinatra: he was speaking about Matt Monro.

Terence Edward Parsons was born in Shoreditch, London, on December 1 1930, the youngest of five children. His father died when he was only three and, when his mother became ill, Terence moved to live with a foster family. Leaving school at the age of 14, he did a series of menial jobs before entering the British army at the age of 17½ years. Two years later he volunteered for overseas duty, and was posted to Hong Kong as a tank driving instructor. Having previously sung at his local dance hall in North London, he continued to sing during his army service in the Far East. There, he entered many talent competitions and became such a frequent winner that he was barred from entering again. In compensation, he was given his own radio show, *Terry Parsons Sings.*

On leaving the army in 1953, he became a bus driver in London. After his day job, Terence sang with dance bands, using the names Terry Fitzgerald and Al Jordan. He also made demo records of new songs for music publishers in Denmark Street, London. A record of "Polka Dots and Moonbeams" that he had made on an earlier trip to Glasgow was heard by the famous pianist Winifred Atwell and was passed by her to Decca, who auditioned Terence, then promptly gave him a recording contract. His name was changed to Matt Monro around that time. As well as appearing on Radio Luxembourg, he also sang with the BBC Show Band, and on Winifred Atwell's television show. Commercial jingles featured prominently in Matt's life; he recorded over 40 for radio and TV advertisements in 12 years.

George Martin, the famous EMI producer, asked Matt to record a demo in the style of Sinatra, to be used as a guide for Peter Sellers to copy, for his next album, *Songs For Swinging Sellers* (1959). A change of plan saw it included, unchanged, on the album with the singer being credited as 'Fred Flange'. Martin then signed Matt to the Parlophone label, a move that soon produced Matt's major hit, "Portrait Of My Love" in 1960. The next six years saw the label issue Matt's 19 singles, eight EPs and four albums. Hits such as "My Kind Of Girl", "From Russia With Love", "Softly As I Leave You", "Born Free" and the

CROONER *Legends*

CROONER *Legends*

atmospheric, "Walk Away" enhanced Monro's reputation internationally, and led to him signing for Capitol in the US, when the label sought a big name after the death of Nat King Cole in 1965.

Matt moved to America where he appeared at major venues, including several Las Vegas casinos, and on many top television shows. His following in Latin America led to him recording the first of many albums in Spanish, one of which went platinum, Matt's first. On returning to the UK, Matt was signed by Columbia and made more hit records, alongside his TV appearances, cabaret tours and theatre shows.

Few at the time new that Matt was an alcoholic. Despite the efforts of his manager Don Black, the addiction continued, as did his heavy smoking. On stage, Matt was the consummate professional, his performances giving no indication of his predilection for strong drink, although it began to affect his health. His last single, "And You Smiled" (1973) entered the Top 30. A 1980 compilation album *Heartbreakers* went gold within a few days after release. By this time Matt was becoming very ill, his liver ravaged by alcohol; he was persuaded that a transplant was the only option. During the surgical operation it was discovered that he had cancer, which had reached an advanced stage, so the transplant was abandoned.

Matt discharged himself from hospital and resumed his stage performances. His recording career was over but he wanted to continue singing for his fans while he was able. His final performance took place in the Barbican Centre, London. The sell-out audience and media critics alike were impressed by the performance that ended with an emotional Matt receiving a poignant, seven-minute standing ovation.

Matt Monro died at the age of 54, in the Cromwell Hospital, London, on February 7 1985. Arguably, Britain's finest ballad singer, the man who was many times voted Britain's No 1 vocalist, was gone. His voice lives on in his legacy of many wonderful recordings.

LEFT

Matt Monro in jovial mood at the 1966 Royal Variety Performance, alongside Sammy Davis Jr and Des O'Connor.

BELOW

Matt Monro on stage in the 1960s.

CROONER *Legends*

FRANK
SINATRA

Birth name: Francis Albert Sinatra
Born: December 12 1915, Paterson Hospital, New Jersey
Died: May 14 1998, Los Angeles, California
Years active: 1930s – 1990s
Record label(s): Columbia, RCA Victor, Capitol, Reprise

"The thing that influenced me most was the way Tommy (Dorsey) played his trombone. It was my idea to make my voice work in the same way as a trombone or violin – not sounding like them, but 'playing' the voice like those instrumentalists." – Frank Sinatra. The man known as 'The Chairman of The Board', also said, "Throughout my career, if I have done anything, I have paid attention to every note and every word I sing - if I respect the song. If I cannot project this to a listener, I fail."

Francis Albert Sinatra, the man who sold over 250 million records and became one of the most influential entertainment figures in the twentieth century, was born in a Paterson, New Jersey, hospital. His parents were both immigrant Italians, father Anthony Sinatra was a boiler-man and his mother Natalie 'Dolly' Garaventa Sinatra, a midwife and part-time Democratic Party ward organiser. Frank was brought up in a relatively comfortable middle class family in Hoboken, New Jersey. In 1935, he was in a group called the Hoboken Four that won a local talent show, the prize being a tour with the promoter. After working as a waiter and singing at clubs, Frank was heard on the radio by bandleader Harry James, who hired him; they made their first record together in July 1939. By the end of that year, Frank had joined Tommy Dorsey and, in 1940, reached No 1 on the Billboard charts with "I'll Never Smile Again". Unfit for military service due to a damaged eardrum at birth, the Sinatra career, both on records with Columbia, and on radio, progressed as a solo artist with Frank making many great recordings.

By the late 1940s, Sinatra had lost favour with his mainly teenage fans, and also damaged his image in a series of public altercations, particularly one in which he punched a journalist. After some lean years, Sinatra began to make a big impact as a movie actor, notably in *From Here To Eternity* (1953), winning Best Supporting Actor at the Academy Awards, and in *The Man With The Golden Arm* (1955) that saw him nominated for Best Actor.

He switched labels to Capitol in 1953, resulting in notable successes with the more upbeat albums such as *Songs For Swinging Lovers*, and hit singles that dominated the charts for four years. Networked television shows and cinema films helped his annual income rise to $4 million. The 1960 founding of his own Reprise label during the Rat Pack years, and a friendship with President John F Kennedy that brought allegations of Mafia involvement in JFK's primary elections, kept the often controversial Sinatra in the public domain. Several of his family members had connections with some high-profile gangsters;

CROONER *Legends*

this led to JFK distancing his presidency from Frank, who later supported the Republican campaign of Nixon.

By 1970, Frank was contemplating retirement but made several 'comeback' appearances on the road, often playing to larger audiences than had frequented the Las Vegas casinos he had played in for many years. In the 1980 presidential elections he threw his support, plus around $4 million, behind the Reagan campaign, later calling in the favour of the elected Reagan as a character reference, to offset the allegations of Sinatra's Mafia connections, in Sinatra's application for a Nevada casino licence.

The same year found Frank releasing his first album for six years, *Trilogy: Past Present Future.* Controversy came with Frank's $2 million contract to sing at Sun City, South Africa, during apartheid, in 1981. This was curiously at odds with his stance against segregation in the US, where he was a leader, together with Sammy Davis, Jr, in the fight to break down racial intolerance in clubs and at casino venues.

Honours came thick and fast for Frank: the Kennedy Center Honor in 1983, the Presidential Medal of Freedom in 1965, and an Honorary Doctor of Engineering degree, which met with protests from students, at his home town Institute of Technology. Frank kept working up to the early 1990s; his two *Duets* albums sold millions of copies. A richly deserved *Grammy* Lifetime Achievement Award complemented a career total of 10 Grammys in 1994.

Sinatra was married four times, to Nancy Barbato, Ava Gardner, Mia Farrow and Barbara Marx, and had other romantic attachments including Lauren Bacall. He had three children, Nancy, Frank, Jr and Christina, all of whom he adored. By his early 80s, most of Frank's friends had passed on; the loss of his friend Dean Martin hit him hard. After suffering a stroke and two heart attacks, Frank Sinatra passed away on May 14 1998. He was buried close to his Rancho Mirage property, near Palm Springs, allegedly wearing a blue suit, and with a bottle of Jack Daniels, a pack of Camel cigarettes, and a Zippo lighter. Ol' Blue Eyes finally did it 'His' Way.

LEFT

Frank Sinatra on tour in 1976.

BELOW

Frank Sinatra in a promotional portrait for one of his many films.

CROONER *Legends*

RUDY VALLEE

Birth name: Hubert Prior Vallee
Born: July 28 1901, Island Pond, Vermont
Died: July 3 1986, Hollywood, California
Years active: 1920s — 1970s
Record label(s): Velvet Tone Records (1928-33), Viva, ABM*, Pearl Flapper*, RKO Unique Records*
(*recent re-releases)

A man with a reputation for being arrogant, egotistical and hot tempered would seem an unlikely candidate to become a popular music and film idol. He was reputed to have been very difficult to work for and was occasionally stricken with stage fright. At times, after he had abandoned his trade mark megaphone for the electric microphone, he was known to have turned his back on his audience and sang facing the band. His temper got the better of him on several occasions when he left the stage to punch a member of the audience who had failed to appreciate his greatness and had heckled him.

Some music historians claim that Vallee, not Gene Austin, was the first of the 'crooners'. He could well have been so, although his continued use of the megaphone after the general adoption of the microphone may have led some to form an incorrect conclusion. His recording career was much less prolific than that of Austin, but he was a major performer on radio, in theatres and later, in the movies, a heartthrob who made the flappers of the day swoon wherever he appeared. Rudy Vallee was born Hubert Prior Vallee on July 28 1901, in Island Pond, Vermont, and grew up in Westbrook, Maine. Vallee adopted the nickname Rudy after his idol, saxophonist Rudy Weidtoft. He took up the saxophone and clarinet while at high school, and also learned to play the drums: these musical skills were put to use in his youth, playing with bands around the New England area.

In 1917, Rudy volunteered for the US Navy but was discharged when they discovered he was underage. He found a job as a movie projectionist before entering the University of Maine in 1921. The following autumn, he transferred to Yale University, studying languages and philosophy, paying his fees and living expenses by playing in country clubs and at dances. He joined the Yale Collegians band and began to sing, using a megaphone to enhance his voice. Vallee dropped out of Yale in 1924 and went to London for a year, where he played saxophone with the Savoy Hotel band.

After returning to Yale, he took his degree in philosophy, and played in the college marching band. After graduation, Rudy went first to Boston and then New York, where he joined an orchestra. He later met Bert Lown, a bandleader, who set up a group fronted by Vallee, which made its debut at the Heigh-Ho Club in January 1928. This band consisted of two violins, two saxophones and a piano; they played only choruses, with Vallee singing songs in several Latin languages through his megaphone.

Radio dates soon followed and Vallee's fame and fortune began to grow, along with his ego: a one-year long theatre tour for Paramount earned him $12,500, a considerable

income in the time of the Great Depression. His popularity soared, leading to his first film in 1929, *The Vagabond Love,* and his own radio series, as host, on *The Fleischmann's Yeast Musical Variety Hour.* Radio engagements lasted well into the 1940s. With his band, The Connecticut Yankees, he made recordings of "The Stein Song", a University song from Maine, and "Vieni, Vieni" toward the end of the 1930s. The band also made numerous live performances in which Rudy continued to delight his largely female audiences; his good looks and light tenor voice, which developed into a baritone in later years, made him the most sought after singer in the US for many years.

Film work continued, the 1942 comedy *The Palm Beach Story* being acclaimed as one of his best, along with another comedy role in the 1955 release *Gentlemen Marry Brunettes.* The 1943 recording of "As Time Goes By", his last major hit, was made while he performed with the Coast Guard Band, entertaining US troops. Further acting success on the Broadway stage, in shows like *How To Succeed In Business Without Really Trying* was rewarded with a role in the film version. In the 60s, Rudy appeared in the Batman television series, and made guest appearances on celebrity shows, while his work in films continued until the 1970s.

Rumoured to have been bisexual, he was married four times; his second wife was the young actress Jane Greer. Rudy also had a much-publicised affair with actress Hedy Lamarr and, as his ego led him to disclose, at least 144 other starlets. He married his last wife, Eleanor Norris, in 1946; this marriage endured until Vallee's death in 1986. Eleanor later wrote her memoirs entitled *My Vagabond Lover* in which she gives a biographical insight into the life of one of the most famous American entertainers of all time.

Rudy Vallee died at the age of 84 while watching a television show. His fame was such that his headstone was stolen from the cemetery at Westbrook in Maine.

CROONER *Legends*

SCOTT
WALKER

Birth name: Noel Scott Engel
Born: January 9 1943
Years active: 1958 – present
Record label(s): Tower, Universal, Philips, Columbia, Virgin, Fontana, Mercury, 4AD

Scott Walker is a musical enigma. First, a solo artist and teen idol, and later becoming a member of a group that achieved massive popularity by singing melodic popular ballads. Then, a solo career that saw him gradually shift away from the popular songs that had made him an international star, as part of The Walker Brothers, into a more soulful and self-indulgent style that encompassed the works of Jacques Brel. His albums of mostly self-written songs with thought-provoking lyrics and a darker musical feel alienated him from his original fan base. Walker has admitted complacency in his choice of material, and the over-reliance on slow tempo in his albums.

Noel Scott Engel was born on January 9 1943 in Hamilton, Ohio, but grew up in New York. Scott's childhood ambition was to become an actor, although music was to become the new direction in his life. He became an accomplished bass guitar player and also recorded under the name Scotty Engel. After moving to Hollywood, he worked as a session bassist before joining a band called The Routers. It was not long before Scott teamed up with another singer, John Maus, and the duo appeared as The Dalton Brothers; they were soon joined by drummer Gary Leeds and the trio became The Walker Brothers.

After crossing the Atlantic in 1965, the group regularly made it to the top of the British charts over the next two years. A rich baritone voice and a stylish, but enigmatic stage persona helped Scott to become popular; his somewhat reclusive choice of lifestyle did not endear him to his manager, Maurice King, who wanted him to exploit his popularity. The Walker Brothers split up in 1967 when Scott, the principal songwriter, grew tired of the concept and had started writing songs for his own future solo performance. The Scott Walker phenomenon seemed almost unstoppable: his first four albums reached the UK Top 10; the second album reached the coveted No 1 position in the 1968 charts. His recordings included a mixture of self-composed material, middle of the road standards, and the more avant garde works of the Belgian composer, Jacques Brel. One of his Brel songs, "Jackie", contained the words "…authentic queers" and other 'unsuitable' references, and was promptly banned by the, then, almost puritanical BBC, thus reducing its exposure to the record buying public of the day.

His fourth album, *Scott 4*, was notable in that it contained only songs written by the performer: its impact was devalued by the almost simultaneous release, by the BBC, of the album *Scott Sings Songs From His Television Series*. Sales of his solo album were adversely affected, and Scott became more downbeat about the progress and direction of his career.

CROONER *Legends*

In 1970, Walker released one of his more critically acclaimed albums, *'Til The Band Comes In*, which stood the test of time and was re-released in 1996. The 1972 album, *The Moviegoer*, consisted entirely of film themes and soundtrack songs, including "Speak Softly Love" from *The Godfather*. His 1973 album *Stretch* was a collection of country songs followed by *We Had It All* a year later. A brief resurrection of The Walker Brothers, in 1975, spawned three albums that were moderately successful: the first single release, "No Regrets" rose to the No 7 position in the UK charts.

After the Walker Brothers last album in 1978, six years elapsed before Scott released the 1984 solo album *Climate of Hunter*. This recording reflected the contemporary music style and, curiously, four of its tracks bore only the track number as their title, "Track Three" being an example: this album was re-released in January 2006. Another decade passed before Walker's next offering, *Tilt* in 1995, in which Scott recorded his vocals once only for each track, with no retakes, over the previously recorded musical backing that included the Sinfonia Strings of London, and a church pipe organ.

The soundtrack album *Pola X*, from the eponymous French film, emerged in 1999, which Scott wrote and also produced. With further soundtrack credits in *To Have And To Hold* and the James Bond film *The World Is Not Enough*, in which he sang "Only Myself To Blame", the career of Scott Walker began to move onward. Around the turn of the millennium he became influential in the career of the pop group Pulp, and produced their album *We Love Life* that was released in 2001. Honoured in 2003 for his contribution to music by the magazine *Q*, only the third to receive such an award, Walker received a standing ovation at the presentation ceremony.

4AD Records released Scott's first album for 11 years in 2006, entitled *Drift*, to critical acclaim and it remained in the album charts for several months. A documentary film, *Scott Walker: 30 Century Man*, was shown as part of the 50th London Film Festival.

ANDY
WILLIAMS

Birth name: Howard Andrew Williams
Born: December 3 1927, Wall Lake, Iowa
Years active: Late 1930s – present
Record label(s): RCA Victor X, Cadence Records, Columbia, Varese

Andy Williams first sang in public at the age of eight years, in a quartet with his three older brothers. His singing career has extended into the 2000s, making regular appearances in his own theatre, The Andy Williams Moon River Theater, in Branson, Missouri, which he built in 1992. A modest and self-effacing man who, in a career that has earned him 18 gold album awards and three platinum records, once said, "I still don't think I'm as good as anyone else."

Howard Andrew Williams was born on December 3 1927 in Wall Lake, Iowa, youngest of four boys. The Williams Brothers Quartet sang with the local church choir, and soon became established favourites on local radio in nearby Des Moines, and later in Chicago and Cincinatti, where Andy attended high school. The quartet was spotted by Bing Crosby, who included the boys on his 1944 hit single, "Swinging On A Star". Their fame spread with appearances in two 1944 films, *Janie* and *Kansas City Kitty,* and two more musical films in 1947, *Something In The Wind* and *Ladies' Man.* Work on the cabaret circuit, with singer Kay Thompson in 1947, continued until the quartet dissolved their act in 1951, when Andy decided to seek his solo singing fortune in New York.

A recording contract in 1952, with RCA Victor's X label, yielded six singles that failed to trouble the chart lists. Andy was given a regular spot on Steve Allen's *Tonight* television show in 1955, the year he was also signed to the small, New York based, Cadence Records label. This contract was the catalyst to Andy's recording success: the third release in 1956, "Canadian Sunset," entered the Top 10 charts, followed by his only *Billboard* No1 hit, "Butterfly", and another Top 10 hit, "I Like Your Kind of Love." Further chart entries were achieved by "The Hawaiian Wedding Song," "Are You Sincere," "The Village of St Bernadette," and "Lonely Street," before Andy moved to Los Angeles in 1961, to sign for Columbia.

The Columbia contract was the biggest recording contract ever awarded to a solo artist up until that time. Andy's albums could hardly fail to hit the charts: "Moon River" and "Days Of Wine and Roses", the second of which reached No 1 chart position in 1963, and stayed there for 16 weeks, are testimony to his popularity. Many more of his albums reached the charts in the 1960s and early 70s, earning 17 of his gold discs by 1973. Williams was also asked to sing at three Oscar ceremonies in 1962, when he sang "Moon River," and again in 1966 and 67, on each occasion performing songs by Henry Mancini. Although considered to be primarily an album artist, Andy also hit the singles charts with

CROONER *Legends*

such unforgettable songs as "Can't Get Used to Losing You," "Happy Heart," and, in 1970, the theme from the film *Love Story*, "Where Do I Begin." Andy has also made a total of eight Christmas albums.

In television, Andy's guest appearances on the *Tonight* shows led to an almost inevitable series of his own in 1962, *The Andy Williams Show*, which won three Emmy Awards for the best variety show. The series ran for almost 10 years before Williams decided to quit at the top of his popularity, and limited his television appearances to three 'specials' per year. He also made a large number of concert tours over the years. Apart from a series of half-hour shows in 1976-77, he kept to the three shows a year format on an occasional basis until the 1990s, before giving up touring and regular television appearances to devote his energies to opening his own theatre in Branson, Missouri.

Far from slowing down his schedule, Andy continued to appear in as many as 12 shows a week in his theatre each autumn, and made the occasional European tour. In 2002, Andy recorded a duet version of his hit, "Can't Take My Eyes Off You," with the British performer, Denise Van Outen.

Andy was twice married, first to singer and ex-Folies Bergère dancer, Claudine Longet, in 1961 with whom he had three children. After their divorce in 1975, Andy supported his ex-wife when she was charged with the 1976 murder of her partner, the ski-star Vladmir Sabich, and shielded their children from the publicity surrounding the event. His second, and enduring marriage, to Debbie Haas, took place in 1991. The Williams live together in Branson, Missouri, and also have a home in La Quinta, California.

Like many entertainers, Andy is a golf fan and hosted the Andy Williams San Diego Open for many years. He is also an avid collector of modern art. Most of his vast catalogue of music is available on compilation albums, the astute Andy having obtained the master tapes of his Cadence recordings, some of which were re-released in the 1990s.

LEFT
Andy Williams performs with dancers on 'The Andy Williams Show' in the 1960s.

BELOW
Andy Williams performing in the 1970s.

CROONER *Legends*

ALSO AVAILABLE IN THIS SERIES

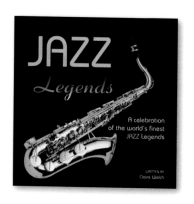

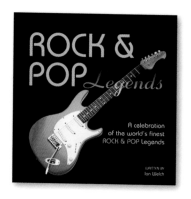

THE PICTURES IN THIS BOOK WERE PROVIDED COURTESY OF THE FOLLOWING:

GETTYIMAGES
101 Bayham Street, London NW1 0AG

Concept and Creative Direction:
VANESSA and KEVINGARDNER

Design and Artwork: KEVINGARDNER

Image research: ELLIECHARLESTON

PUBLISHED BY GREEN UMBRELLA PUBLISHING

Publishers:
JULESGAMMOND and VANESSAGARDNER

Written by: DAVIDCURNOCK